CY COLEMAN
ANTHOLOGY

Cover photo (1986) © Nevin Shalit
Used by Permission

All materials courtesy of Notable Music Co. Inc./The Cy Coleman Office

ISBN 978-1-4234-6513-3

HAL•LEONARD®
CORPORATION
7777 W. BLUEMOUND RD. P.O. BOX 13819 MILWAUKEE, WI 53213

Visit Hal Leonard Online at
www.halleonard.com

www.cycoleman.com
www.notablemusic.net

CY COLEMAN

In any field of human endeavor, it falls to a select few to set the standard; an even fewer who become the standard. For inclusion in that exclusive circle within the circle, one no bigger than say, an eighth note, allow me to nominate the name of Cy Coleman.

Some folks strike oil. Some strike gold. Cy Coleman struck music. A mother lode. A gusher.

From the time he was knee-high to a Steinway, the piano became Cy's playmate; and his playground. Seated at the grandest of grands or ennobling a broken-down upright, they were all just different sets of ivories for Cy to master and ultimately seduce. The man simply never met a piano he couldn't sweep off its legs.

As a composer, there was a deep, mysterious place inside his being that kept harvesting bar after bar of tune after tune, each unmistakably written in the key of Cy, his musical gyroscope allowing him to compose melodies that pleased as much as they teased; songs that amused as often as they amazed.

It was as though Cy, the composer, aided by Cy, the pianist, knew where certain, extra notes were hidden among the mere 88 available to the rest of us.

With 26 musical shows and hundreds and hundreds of songs to his credit, Cy was hardly an unsung hero. Why, some wondered, didn't he ever cool it and just sit back on his ASCAP? The answer was quite simple: if Cy Coleman refused to rest on his laurels it could only have been because he was afraid of heights.

Certain of his tunes have the zing and snap of musical martinis, sounding as though Fred Astaire might have composed them by somehow tap dancing atop a keyboard. The sly nonchalance with which Cy imbued his compositions gave the impression that, acting as a thoughtful host, he really knew how to turn a song into a party, introducing one note to another for the very first time.

His laid-back style belied the non-stop workings of a mind that was constantly in overdrive, one forever playing multi-dimensional, musical chess. His was a head jammed full of ideas, always skipping from one venture to another: a new show score he was working on—or three—or maybe four (a master juggler, he was forever pollinating new projects whenever any one particular work teetered perilously close to completion), or augmenting the score of a revival of one of his earlier hits—or two or more (his was a gift that kept on re-giving), or else he was off to concertize somewhere or picking up yet another award—or twelve.

If any of this borders on hyperbole, be assured that Cy Coleman was never burdened by modesty; he was never one to be held prisoner by any sort of false pride. His was the real kind. In any case, his work has earned him the right to an endless amount of posthumous preening. In the end, his songs will act as the keepers of his fame.

Overhead, in the caves at Lascaux, in France, are the famous handprints pressed indelibly onto the ceiling, handprints left countless millennia ago by a primitive people who wanted to say to ages yet unborn: "We were here."

What Cy Coleman leaves behind for those yet to come is a message that says that there were once among us—way, way back in what we in our time call "now"—a precious few talented souls who had the ability to marry sound with emotion, and, by doing so, creating a language that was far superior to mere words.

"We were here," Cy's song-prints will tell them in the countless notes with which he graced our culture. We were here and we never stopped reaching for the stars, or for the clutch and comfort of another person's hand. That we spent as much time stumbling as we did getting back up on our feet; and when tears weren't an option, we laughed our way back to equilibrium.

Surely, what lies ahead for Cy's music is an eternity of replays, a never-ending reprise of his songs to delight the ear and refresh the heart, right up until the moment that this fevered planet finally cools—just before it shrinks to say, the size of an eighth note.

© LARRY GELBART
Beverly Hills 2009

Cy as an infant

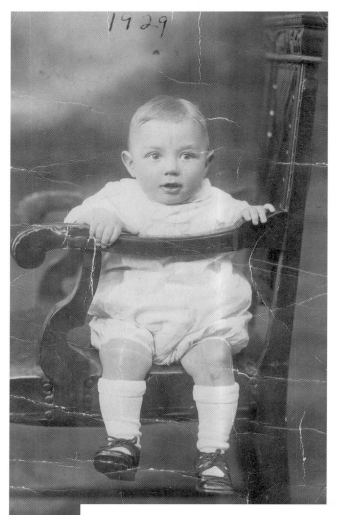

Cy as an 8-year-old street tough

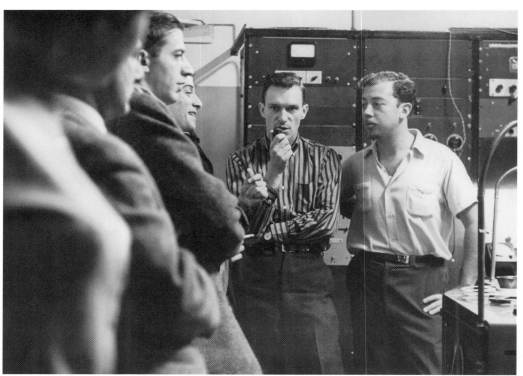

Cy (on right) with Hugh Hefner, 1959

When you and I were babes... Remember? Love, Carolyn

Cy with Carolyn Leigh, 1960

An early publicity shot, 1958

PHOTO: LESTER L. KRAUSS

Cy with Duke Ellington, 1955

PHOTO: DAVID WORKMAN

*Between takes for the original Broadway cast recording of Sweet Charity, 1966: Goddard Lieberson (producer);
Cy; Fred Werner (music director); Dorothy Fields (lyricist); Gwen Verdon (Charity); Bob Fosse (choreographer).*

PHOTO: © DON HUNSTEIN

Cy with Johnny Mercer in 1967 testifying on Capitol Hill regarding copyright extension.

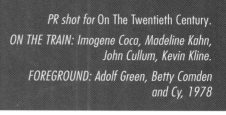

PR shot for On The Twentieth Century.
ON THE TRAIN: Imogene Coca, Madeline Kahn, John Cullum, Kevin Kline.
FOREGROUND: Adolf Green, Betty Comden and Cy, 1978

Tony Bennett, Chita Rivera and Cy, circa 1970

Cy, wife Shelby, and 7-month-old daughter Lily Cy Coleman, 2000.

*The finale from the 1986 Tony® Awards.
Cy at the piano, singing
"You There in the Back Row."*

Cy in 1980

Cy performing with Ira Gasman, 1997
PHOTO: TED CURRY

Cy, Paul McCartney, Carly Simon, Linda McCartney, 1989

Cy in 1997

CONTENTS

BABY DREAM YOUR DREAM

from SWEET CHARITY

Music by CY COLEMAN
Lyrics by DOROTHY FIELDS

BIG SPENDER
from SWEET CHARITY

Music by CY COLEMAN
Lyrics by DOROTHY FIELDS

BE A PERFORMER

from LITTLE ME

Music by CY COLEMAN
Lyrics by CAROLYN LEIGH

THE BEST IS YET TO COME

Music by CY COLEMAN
Lyrics by CAROLYN LEIGH

Moderately, with a beat

Out of the tree of life ___ I just picked me a plum. ___

You came a-long and ev-'ry-thing's start-in' to

hum. ___ Still it's a real good bet ___

CITY OF ANGELS - THEME

from CITY OF ANGELS

Music by CY COLEMAN
Lyrics by DAVID ZIPPEL

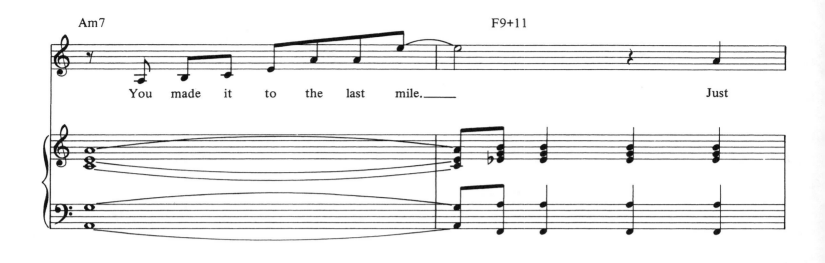

You made it to the last mile.____ Just

puck-er up, suck-er, and kiss your ass____ good-bye.____

THE COLORS OF MY LIFE
from BARNUM

Music by CY COLEMAN
Lyrics by MICHAEL STEWART

The Col - ors Of My Life _____ are boun - ti - ful and bold, _____

The pur - ple glow of in - di - go _____ the gleam of green and

COME FOLLOW THE BAND

from BARNUM

Music by CY COLEMAN
Lyrics by MICHAEL STEWART

HEY THERE, GOOD TIMES

from I LOVE MY WIFE

Music by CY COLEMAN
Lyrics by MICHAEL STEWART

Moderately, with a lift

Bb6

Hey There Good Times, here I am.___ Wel - come back your ba - by lamb.___
Hey There Good Times, let me in.___ Ask me how the hell I been.___

44

FIREFLY

Music by CY COLEMAN
Lyrics by CAROLYN LEIGH

HERE'S TO US

from LITTLE ME

Music by CY COLEMAN
Lyrics by CAROLYN LEIGH

may not be Em-'ly Post to say it, But, here's how! And I must say it:

Refrain-Moderately bright bounce

HERE'S TO US, my dar-ling, my dear,___ HERE'S TO US to - night;___ Not for what might hap-pen next year,__ For it might not be near - ly as bright___

HEY, LOOK ME OVER

from WILDCAT

Music by CY COLEMAN
Lyrics by CAROLYN LEIGH

March tempo

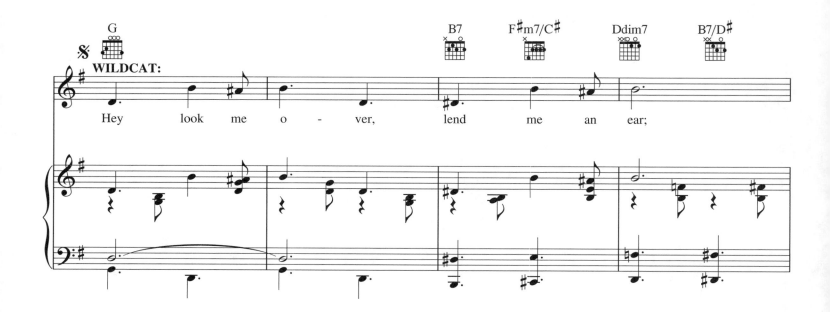

Hey look me o - ver, lend me an ear;

fresh out of clo - ver, mort - gaged up to here. _____ But

Kid, when you need the crowd, the tick - ets are hard to sell;

D.S. al Coda

still you can lead the crowd, if you can get up and yell:

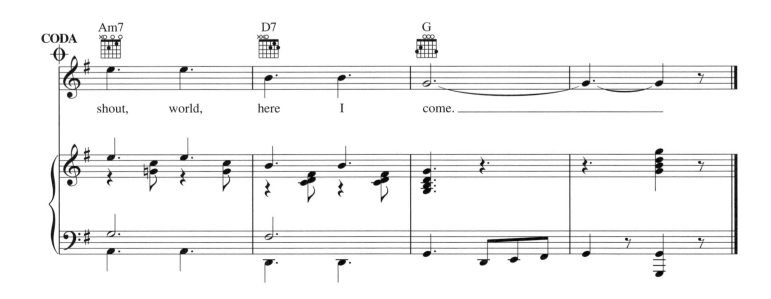

shout, world, here I come.

I LOVE MY WIFE

from I LOVE MY WIFE

Music by CY COLEMAN
Lyrics by MICHAEL STEWART

I WALK A LITTLE FASTER

Music by CY COLEMAN
Lyrics by CAROLYN LEIGH

I'M IN LOVE AGAIN

Words and Music by PEGGY LEE,
CY COLEMAN and BILL SCHLUGER

I'M A BRASS BAND

from SWEET CHARITY

Music by CY COLEMAN
Lyrics by DOROTHY FIELDS

I'M GONNA LAUGH YOU RIGHT OUT OF MY LIFE

Words and Music by JOSEPH McCARTHY
and CY COLEMAN

I'VE GOT YOUR NUMBER

from LITTLE ME

Music by CY COLEMAN
Lyrics by CAROLYN LEIGH

Moderate, with a relaxed swinging beat

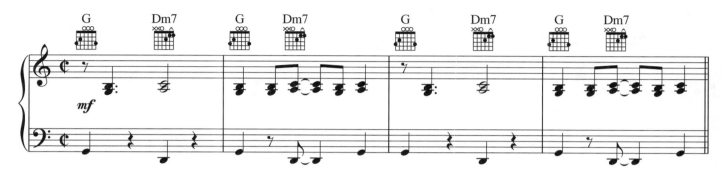

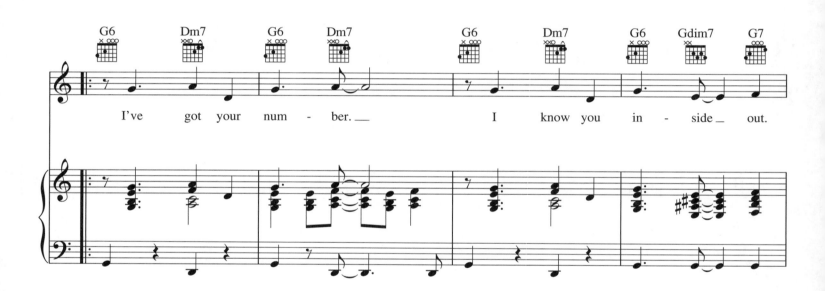

I've got your num-ber. ___ I know you in-side ___ out.

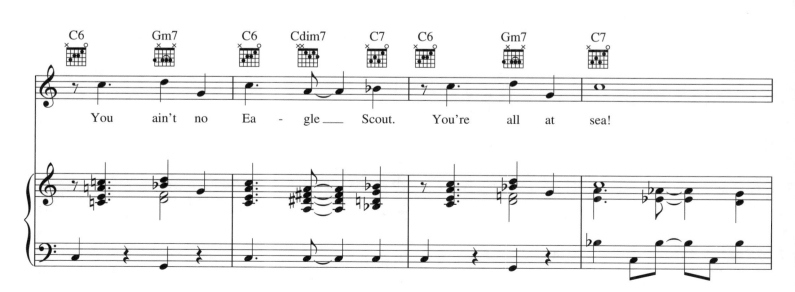

You ain't no Ea - gle ___ Scout. You're all at sea!

IF MY FRIENDS COULD SEE ME NOW

from SWEET CHARITY

Music by CY COLEMAN
Lyrics by DOROTHY FIELDS

IT AMAZES ME

Music by CY COLEMAN
Lyrics by CAROLYN LEIGH

Moderately, With Feeling

Verse

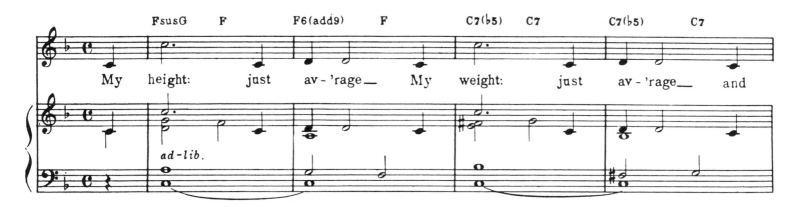

My height: just av-'rage__ My weight: just av-'rage__ and

my I. Q. is__ like you'd es-ti-mate__ just av-'rage__ But

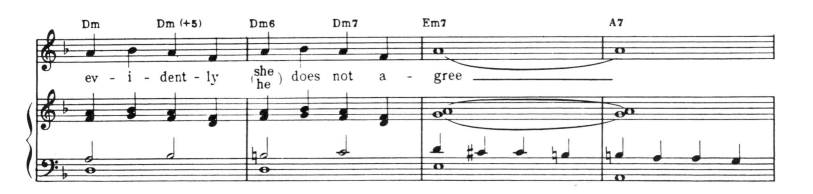

ev-i-dent-ly (she) (he) does not a-gree _____

Con - se - quent - ly if I seem at sea: _____

Chorus Moderately, With Feeling

IT A - MAZ - ES ME _____ It sim - ply a - maz - es me _____ What (she)(he)

sees in me daz - zles me, da - zes me! _____ That I've

learned to clip my wings and sof - ten my ways _____ These are

or - di - nar - y things un - worth - y of praise _____ Yet (she)(he)

IT'S NOT WHERE YOU START

from SEESAW

Music by CY COLEMAN
Lyrics by DOROTHY FIELDS

JOIN THE CIRCUS

from BARNUM

Music by CY COLEMAN
Lyrics by MICHAEL STEWART

A MOMENT OF MADNESS

Music by CY COLEMAN
Lyrics by CAROLYN LEIGH

LITTLE ME

from LITTLE ME

Music by CY COLEMAN
Lyrics by CAROLYN LEIGH

LOST AND FOUND
from CITY OF ANGELS

Music by CY COLEMAN
Lyrics by DAVID ZIPPEL

MY PERSONAL PROPERTY
from the Motion Picture SWEET CHARITY

Music by CY COLEMAN
Lyrics by DOROTHY FIELDS

NEVER MET A MAN I DIDN'T LIKE

from THE WILL ROGERS FOLLIES

Music by CY COLEMAN
Lyrics by BETTY COMDEN and ADOLPH GREEN

NOBODY DOES IT LIKE ME

from SEESAW

Music by CY COLEMAN
Lyrics by DOROTHY FIELDS

THE OTHER SIDE OF THE TRACKS

from LITTLE ME

Music by CY COLEMAN
Lyrics by CAROLYN LEIGH

Deliberate tempo, intense and driving
(not too fast and done with a gradual build)

OUR PRIVATE WORLD
from ON THE TWENTIETH CENTURY

Music by CY COLEMAN and ADOLPH GREEN
Lyrics by BETTY COMDEN and ADOLPH GREEN

Moderately, with expression

Our Pri - vate World _____ is like a play a - bout a pair of lov - ers. The plot says on - ly we may en - ter and

REAL LIVE GIRL

from LITTLE ME

Music by CY COLEMAN
Lyrics by CAROLYN LEIGH

Moderate Waltz

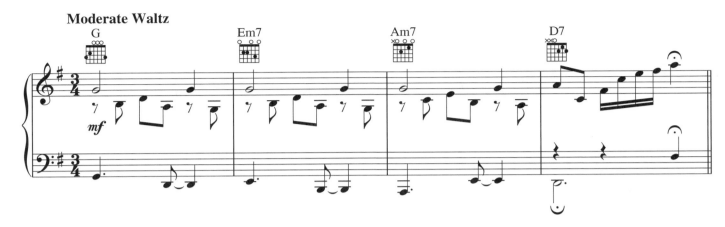

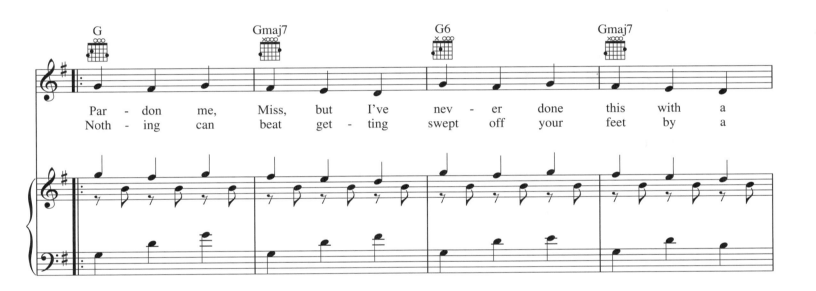

Par - don me, Miss, but I've nev - er done this with a
Noth - ing can beat get - ting swept off done your feet by a

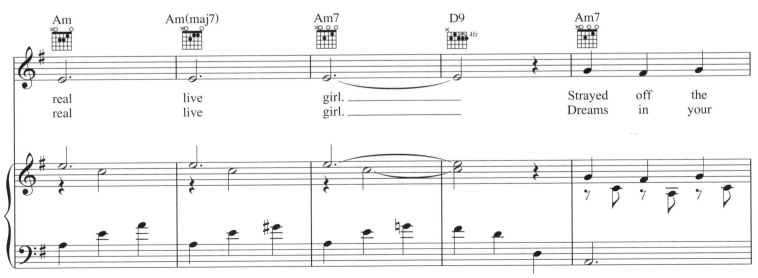

real live girl. _____ Strayed off the
real live girl. _____ Dreams in your

PLAYBOY'S THEME

Music by CY COLEMAN
Lyrics by CAROLYN LEIGH

So she's giv-ing him the razz-a-ma-taz-zle, and he's ob-vi-ous-ly drink-ing it in. ___ He's at-tract-ed to her du-bi-ous daz-zle. That's how it's been ___

POOR EVERYBODY ELSE

from SEESAW

Music by CY COLEMAN
Lyrics by DOROTHY FIELDS

THE RHYTHM OF LIFE
from SWEET CHARITY

Music by CY COLEMAN
Lyrics by DOROTHY FIELDS

*Group E – 1st time through women only (sing top note), 2nd time add men on bottom note harmony (sung at pitch)

Hit the floor and crawl to Dad - dy! Hit the floor and crawl to Dad - dy!

Hit the floor and crawl to Dad - dy! Crawl, __ crawl, __ crawl to Dad - dy!

GROUP A:

And the rhy - thm of life is a pow - er - ful beat, puts a

RULES OF THE ROAD

Music by CY COLEMAN
Lyrics by CAROLYN LEIGH

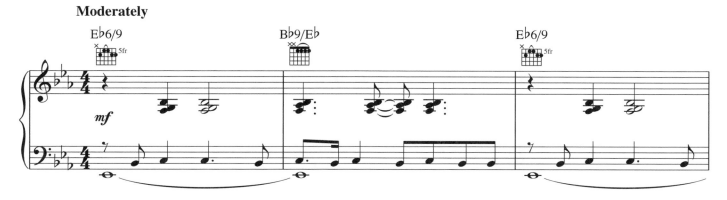

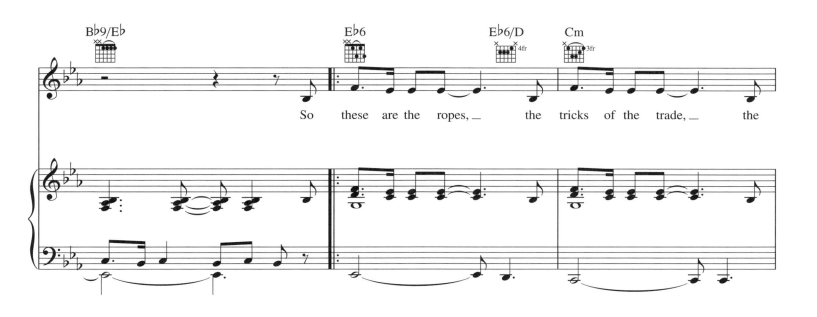

So these are the ropes, __ the tricks of the trade, __ the

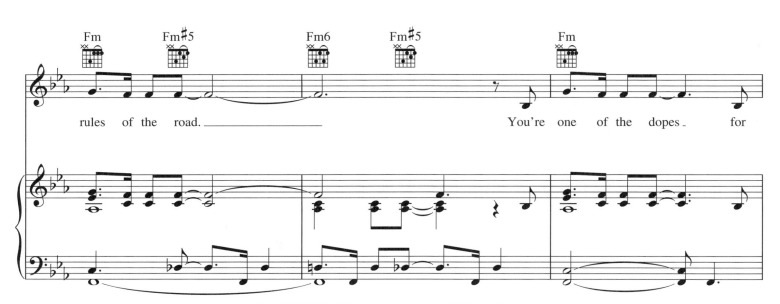

rules of the road. _____ You're one of the dopes __ for

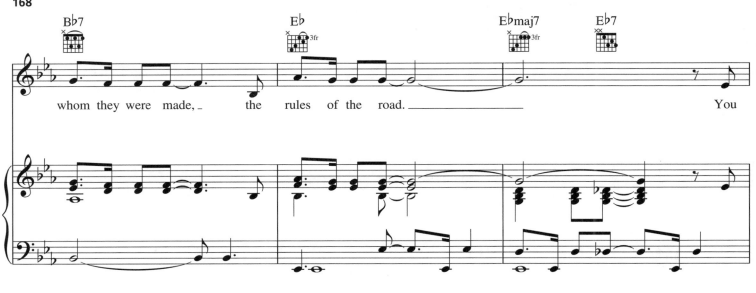

whom they were made, ___ the rules of the road. ___ You

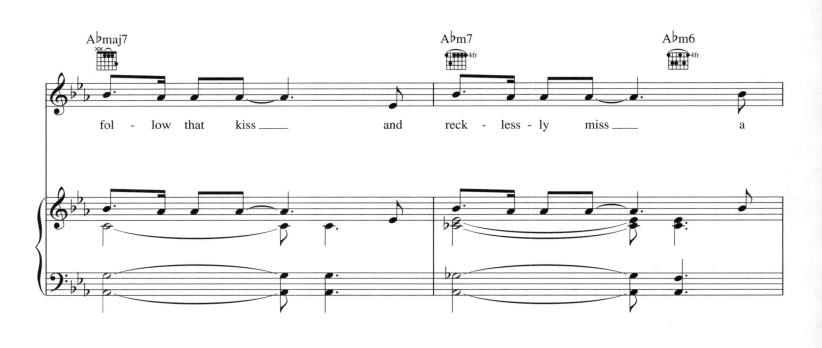

fol - low that kiss ___ and reck - less - ly miss ___ a

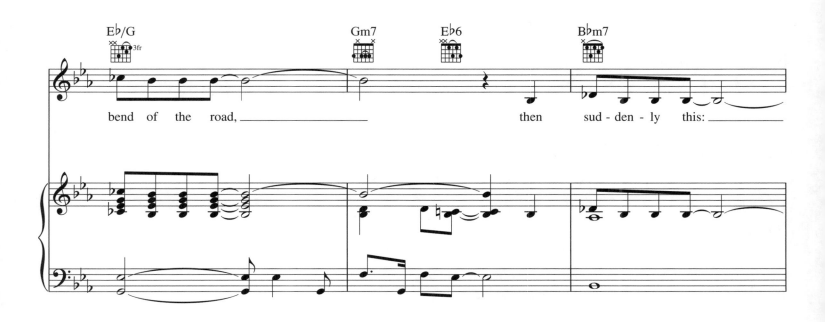

bend of the road, ___ then sud - den - ly this: ___

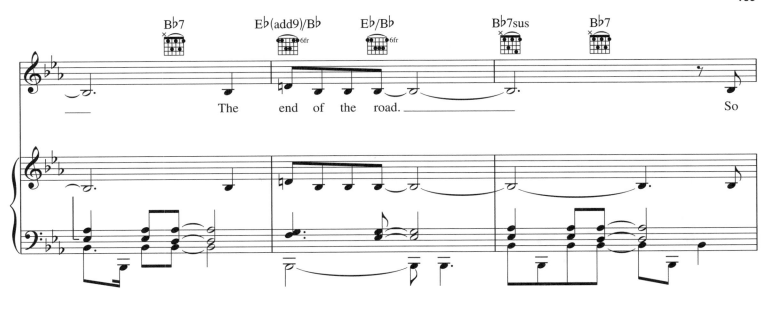

The end of the road. _____ So

love is a hoax, _ a glit-ter-ing string _ of lit-tle white lies, _____

____ but these are the jokes _ and what if they bring _ the

THE RIVIERA

Music by CY COLEMAN and JOSEPH McCARTHY
Lyrics by JOSEPH McCARTHY

SEESAW
from SEESAW

Music by CY COLEMAN
Lyrics by DOROTHY FIELDS

SOUTHERN COMFORT
from WELCOME TO THE CLUB

Music by CY COLEMAN
Lyrics by CY COLEMAN and A.E. HOTCHNER

1. Black- eyed peas, _____ Hon- ey bees, _____
2. Pe- can pies, _____ Sul- try skies, _____
3. Smell of pine, _____ New York wine, _____
4. South- ern Belle, _____ North- ern gent, _____

A la- zy ham- mock swing- in' in the breeze. _____
And sit- tin' on a rock- er swat- tin' flies. _____
When you're a- cross the Ma- son Dix- on line. _____
A com- bin- a- tion that is heav- en sent. _____

SOMEONE WONDERFUL I MISSED

from I LOVE MY WIFE

Music by CY COLEMAN
Lyrics by MICHAEL STEWART

STAY WITH ME

from CITY OF ANGELS

Music by CY COLEMAN
Lyrics by DAVID ZIPPEL

THERE'S GOTTA BE SOMETHING BETTER THAN THIS

from SWEET CHARITY

Music by CY COLEMAN
Lyrics by DOROTHY FIELDS

THEN WAS THEN AND NOW IS NOW

Words and Music by CY COLEMAN
and PEGGY LEE

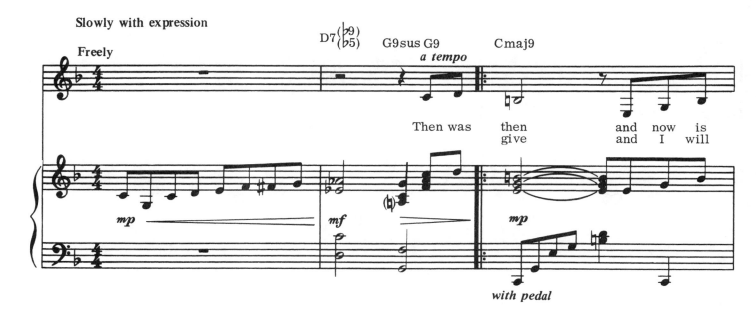

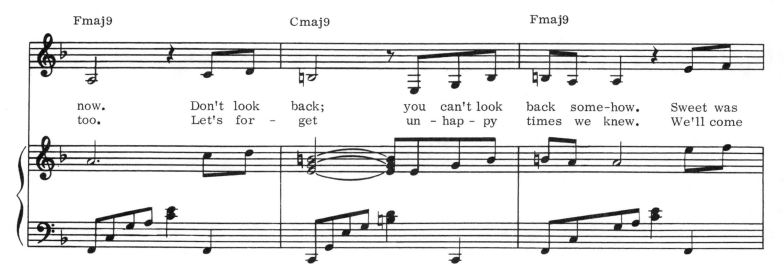

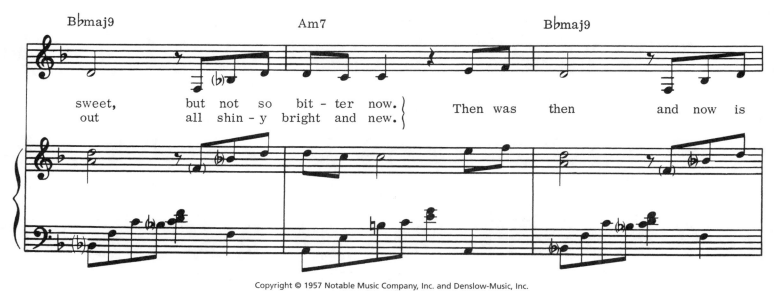

WHEN IN ROME
(I Do as the Romans Do)

Music by CY COLEMAN
Lyrics by CAROLYN LEIGH

Rhythmically

Though now and then your prob-lems fall ___ with-in the er-rant mate de-part - ment, for-get the trans-at - lan - tic call. ___ Don't no-ti-fy the State De-part - ment.

WITCHCRAFT

Music by CY COLEMAN
Lyrics by CAROLYN LEIGH

WHERE AM I GOING

from SWEET CHARITY

Music by CY COLEMAN
Lyrics by DOROTHY FIELDS

Rhythmically

CHARITY:

Where am I go - ing and what will I find? _ What's in this grab _ bag that

I call my mind? _ What am I do - ing a - lone on the shelf? _

WHY TRY TO CHANGE ME NOW?

Words and Music by JOSEPH McCARTHY
and CY COLEMAN

WITH EVERY BREATH I TAKE

from CITY OF ANGELS

Music by CY COLEMAN
Lyrics by DAVID ZIPPEL

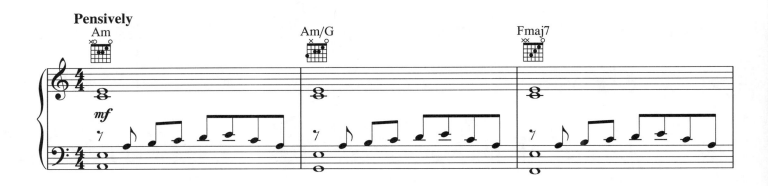

There's not a morn-ing that I o-pen up my eyes

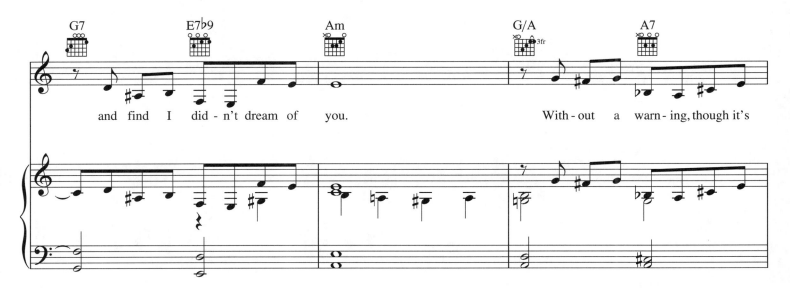

and find I did-n't dream of you. With-out a warn-ing, though it's

YOU CAN ALWAYS COUNT ON ME

from CITY OF ANGELS

Music by CY COLEMAN
Lyrics by DAVID ZIPPEL

I come from a long line of good girls who choose the wrong guy to be sweet on; the girl with a face that says "wel - come" that men can wipe their feet on. I'm there when he calls me, the trust - ed girl Fri - day, al -

right, but what good does it do me a- lone on a Sat-ur-day night?

I don't need a map, I nat -'ral - ly head for the dead end street._
mat - ter of fact, if you want an ill - fat - ed love af - fair, _
my kind of dame no doubt will die out like the di - no - saurs, _

You can al - ways count on me. _____ I'm
you can al - ways count on me. _____ Though
you can al - ways count on me. _____ I'm

YOU THERE IN THE BACK ROW

from 13 DAYS TO BROADWAY

Music by CY COLEMAN
Lyrics by BARBARA FRIED

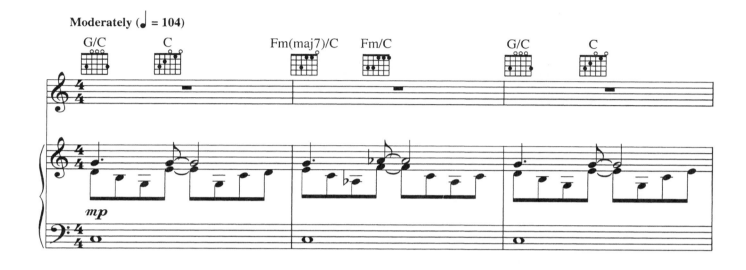

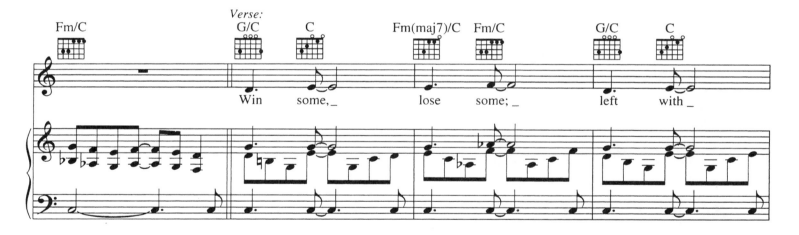

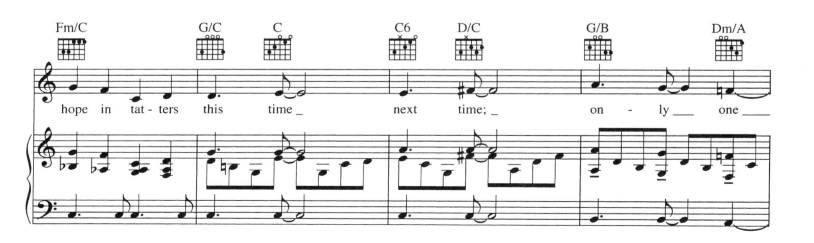

YOU FASCINATE ME SO

Music by CY COLEMAN
Lyrics by CAROLYN LEIGH

Deliberately, With A Steady Beat

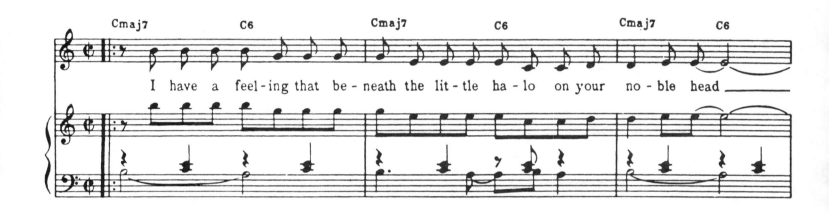

I have a feel-ing that be-neath the lit-tle ha-lo on your no-ble head _____

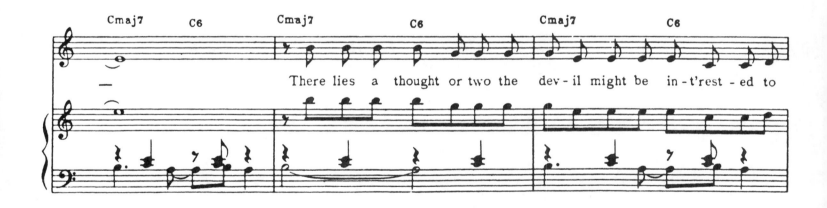

_____ There lies a thought or two the dev-il might be in-t'rest-ed to

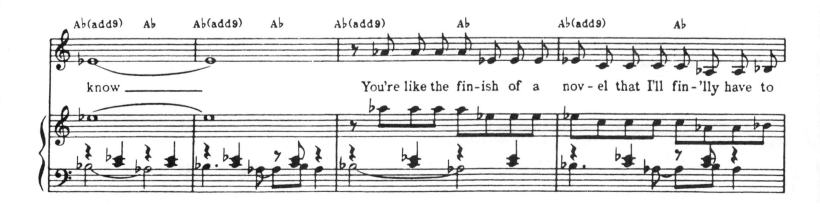

know _____ You're like the fin-ish of a nov-el that I'll fin-'lly have to

YOU'RE NOTHING WITHOUT ME

from CITY OF ANGELS

Music by CY COLEMAN
Lyrics by DAVID ZIPPEL

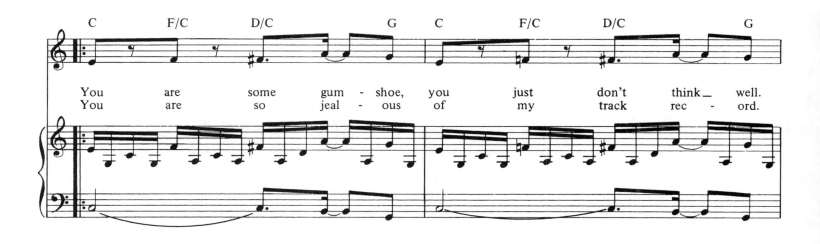

You are some gum-shoe, you just don't think_ well.
You are so jeal-ous of just my track rec - ord.

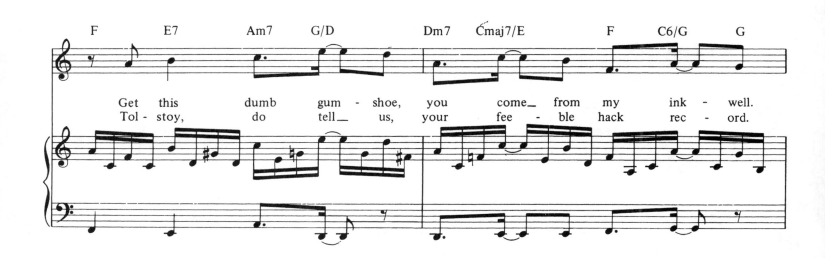

Get this dumb gum-shoe, you come_ from my ink - well.
Tol-stoy, do tell_ us, your fee - ble hack rec - ord.

236

*Alternate lyrics for "YOU'RE NOTHING WITHOUT ME" (If alternate lyrics are used, begin song at this point.)
**Alternate lyrics for "I'M NOTHING WITHOUT YOU"

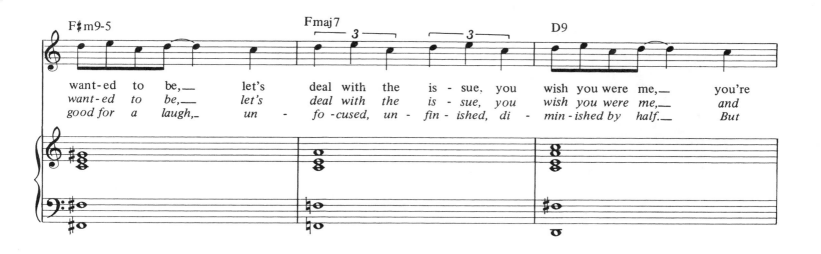

F♯m9-5   **Fmaj7**   **D9**

want-ed   to   be,—   let's   deal   with   the   is - sue,   you   wish   you   were   me,—   you're

want-ed   to   be,—   let's   deal   with   the   is - sue,   you   wish   you   were   me,—   and

good   for   a   laugh,—   un -   fo -cused,   un - fin - ished,   di - min -ished   by   half.—   But

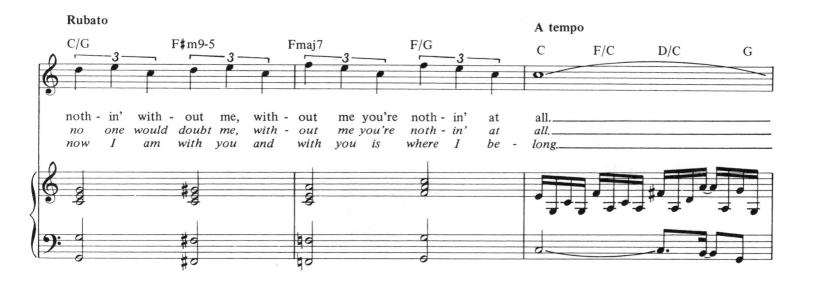

Rubato   **A tempo**

C/G   **F♯m9-5**   **Fmaj7**   **F/G**   **C**   **F/C**   **D/C**   **G**

noth - in'   with - out   me,   with - out   me   you're   noth - in'   at   all._____

no   one   would   doubt   me,   with - out   me   you're   noth - in'   at   all._____

now   I   am   with   you   and   with   you   is   where   I   be - long._____

C   **F/C**   **D/C**   **G**   **F**   **E7**   **Am7**   **G/D**   **Dm7**   **F/G**   **C**

8va- - -

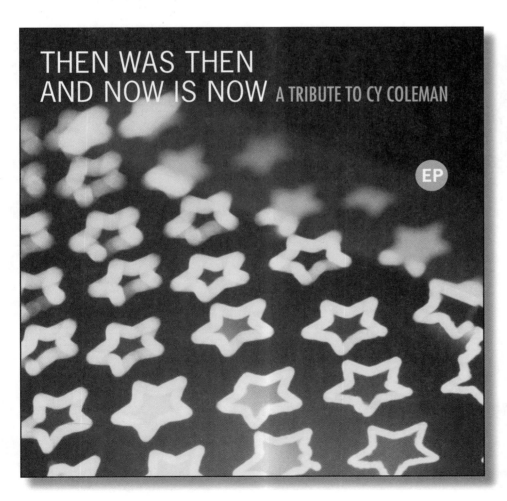